IMPERMANENT WAYS

THE CLOSED LINES OF BRITAIN VOLUME 4

DEVON

Amyas Crump

GW00685556

Noodle Books

© Kevin Robertson (Noodle Books) and Amyas Crump 2012

ISBN 978 1 9064 19 76 9

Printed in England by The Information Press
Designed by Jeremy English
Series Editor Jeffery Grayer
First published in 2012 by Kevin Robertson
under the **NOODLE BOOKS** imprint

PO Box 279, Corhampton, SOUTHAMPTON. SO32 3ZX

www.noodlebooks.co.uk

CONTENTS

Front cover - Passengers no more. With last rites becoming but a memory, the station at Thorverton awaits its fate while the weeds quickly gain a hold and the roses for which the station was so well known are going untended (I am told the key to their success was in the amount of tea drunk by railwaymen and long spells between trains!). General freight had long been concentrated at Exeter - pre-WW2 the yard had been home to a camping coach - an idyllic spot. The private siding to the mill here continued to provide rail traffic until the end of November 1966, the stub of the branch from Stoke Canon Junction operating as a long siding. Traffic ran 'as required' and provided one of the turns for the last few ex-GWR pannier tanks, by then allocated to Exmouth Junction. With the end of the grain traffic, the station was sold off, the station buildings extended as a family size home and the goods yard redeveloped.

Frontispiece - Littleham on the LSWR extension of the original Budleigh Salterton Railway to Exmouth. Following closure in 1966 it now slumbers awaiting replacement by a shopping centre and housing.

Opposite top - No. 1471 waits in Tiverton's bay platform with the 'Tivvy Bumper' shuttle service to the main line at Tiverton Junction in August 1962.Just visible to the left of the engine, the water tank provided a supply to the whole station which was drawn from the nearby canal whilst the station remained gas lit from the formerly rail connected gas works. Across the long through platforms is the roof of the station with its ornate chimney pots, beyond which the avenue of lime trees line the station approach road. To the right of the end tree is the area of the goods yard - also the site of the original terminus.

Rear cover - Finis.

INTRODUCTION

Travelling through Devon on today's railway it is easy to completely miss the many lines and wayside stations that have been swept aside - particularly during the Beeching era. Away from today's operational railway, changes have been dramatic, station sites landscaped or given over to industrial use and later even housing, miles of trackbed now tarmac, cycle paths or even lying fallow.

As closure notices appeared so attempts were made to preserve various, usually with the genuine intention of maintaining a passenger service. Few succeeded, places such as Ilfracombe and Kingsbridge destined to see their road traffic increase whilst their rail service declined.

I was lucky to have seen something of this era of change and be able to explore what had gone before too much had been obliterated. Also, to have met old railwaymen and those with memories of a trip on the last train to Lynton, how we envy them! As always, this book could not have come about without the support and interest of many others, in particular I would like to thank my family. For help with research and photographs, thanks go to Sean Bolan, Colin Burges, Bert Demellweek, Les Foulkard, Peter Gray, Pippa Griffith, Roger Hateley, Chris Henley, John Hill, Carl Honnor, Stewart Hookins, David & Sue Massey, Bernard Mills, Bill Rogers, Alan Sainty, Liz Shepherd, Andrew Snowdon, Peter Triggs, Chris Tilley, Tiverton Museum and Tony Woodforth Also to Jeremy English for layout and design, Jeff Grayer for the opportunity and Kevin Robertson for endless patience and scanning.

Amyas Crump, Exeter, February 2012

By 1976 it must have come as something of a shock to the residents of Up Exe to find the South Crossing gates closed across the road (by a young Amyas!)   (Alice Bellamy)   4

SR FREMINGTON to BARNSTAPLE

FREMINGTON   closed (p) 4-10-65 (g) 31-8-82

Perhaps an unusual place to start a tour of Devon's railways, but appropriate as a tramway from here to Barnstaple was the first 'railway' in North Devon. This charming view on 4 May 1964 by renowned photographer Chris Gammell, has captured a timeless, everyday scene that would soon be gone forever. Today the trackbed is a cycleway.

FREMINGTON QUAY

Left - Although the cranes installed by the SR in the 1930s have no work and the considerable tonnages of clay have gone, the infrastructure of the quay is still all in place, as is the signalbox. Given its height and exposed waterfront position, this must have been a bleak box to work in winter!

Below - A standard gauge horse worked tramway opened to Barnstaple in 1846, becoming part of the 7' 0¼" broad gauge route from Bideford to Cowley Bridge Junction. Once the North Devon Railway was acquired by the LSWR it was converted to the standard gauge.

By June 1984 when this view was taken, activity at the quay had ceased, some of the last traffic being coal to North Yelland Power Station. This traffic was switched to rail/road via the Taunton Coal Concentration Depot - opened to allow withdrawal of service to coal merchants at a number of wayside stations and with it the complete closure of various branch lines. A quarter of a century would pass before Fremington saw another train - and then it was Hornby-size. James May organised a marathon run of a number of Hornby models for a television show in 2009 along the trackbed from Barnstaple to Bideford.
(Tony Woodford).

BARNSTAPLE JUNCTION

The very last-built example of the 140 Bulleid Pacifics, No. 34110, '66 Squadron', rumbles into Barnstaple Junction off the line from Ilfracombe with a fellow Pacific tucked in behind. After the Western Region took over all the former Southern lines west of Exeter from the beginning of 1963, it rapidly phased-out the use of the Southern locomotives. No. 34110 was one of those it inherited at Exmouth Junction shed, but was sent back to Eastleigh for scrapping at the end of November the same year. Soon the lines themselves would go under the torch as the WR pursued a policy both of dieselisation and the reduction of trackwork and branches. The line from Fremington is seen coming in on the left of the picture: it would be the longer-lived of the two lines branching off here at the western end of Barnstaple Junction.

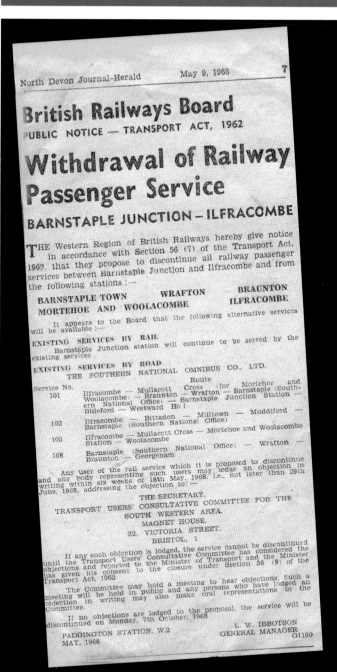

North Devon Journal-Herald   May 9, 1968   7

British Railways Board
PUBLIC NOTICE — TRANSPORT ACT, 1962

Withdrawal of Railway Passenger Service
BARNSTAPLE JUNCTION — ILFRACOMBE

THE Western Region of British Railways hereby give notice in accordance with Section 56 (7) of the Transport Act, 1962, that they propose to discontinue all railway passenger services between Barnstaple Junction and Ilfracombe and from the following stations :—

BARNSTAPLE TOWN   WRAFTON   BRAUNTON
MORTEHOE AND WOOLACOMBE   ILFRACOMBE

It appears to the Board that the following alternative services will be available :—

EXISTING SERVICES BY RAIL
  Barnstaple Junction station will continue to be served by the existing services

EXISTING SERVICES BY ROAD
  THE SOUTHERN NATIONAL OMNIBUS CO., LTD.

Service No.   Route
101   Ilfracombe — Mullacott Cross (for Mortehoe and Woolacombe) — Braunton — Wrafton — Barnstaple (Southern National Office) — Barnstaple Junction Station — Bideford — Westward Ho !
102   Ilfracombe — Bittadon — Milltown — Muddiford — Barnstaple (Southern National Office)
103   Ilfracombe — Mullacott Cross — Mortehoe and Woolacombe Station — Woolacombe
108   Barnstaple (Southern National Office) — Wrafton — Braunton — Georgeham

Any user of the rail service which it is proposed to discontinue and any body representing such users may lodge an objection in writing within six weeks of 18th May, 1968, i.e., not later than 29th June, 1968, addressing the objection to :—

THE SECRETARY,
TRANSPORT USERS' CONSULTATIVE COMMITTEE FOR THE
SOUTH WESTERN AREA,
MAGNET HOUSE,
32, VICTORIA STREET,
BRISTOL, 1

If any such objection is lodged, the service cannot be discontinued until the Transport Users' Consultative Committee has considered the objections and reported to the Minister of Transport and the Minister has given his consent to the closure under Section 56 (8) of the Transport Act, 1962

The Committee may hold a meeting to hear objections. Such a meeting will be held in public and any persons who have lodged an objection in writing may also make oral representations to the Committee.

If no objections are lodged to the proposal, the service will be discontinued on Monday, 7th October, 1968

PADDINGTON STATION, W.2   L. W. IBBOTSON
MAY, 1968   GENERAL MANAGER
                                                    G1190

Closure notice issued from Paddington, '...*if no objections are lodged to the proposal, the service will be discontinued on Monday, 7 October, 1968*'. The first news of closure for many came with the public notice in the press, most of the locals having already abandoned their railway station. A long campaign kept the line alive for another two years, during which time BR removed all the sidings until just a single running line remained. The will of BR alsol prevailed and closure took place from 15 October 1970.

Even so, for some there was still hope and a preservation society raised some £20,000 towards the purchase of the line - a long way short of the BR valuation of £410,000 - not surprisingly the scheme collapsed. Perhaps even with a view to a change of heart a final train ran on 26 February 1975 - a class 25 with an Inspection Saloon took officers to see whether reinstatement was feasible. It wasn't and final lifting took place in June that year.

For Ilfracombe though, like so many resorts, the departure of the last train also brought about the end of much tourism. Ilfracombe remains depressed, although Woolacombe, like Braunton, has developed as a major centre for surfing. The latter also sees considerable usage of a cycleway on the old trackbed.

(North Devon Journal-Herald 9 May 1968)

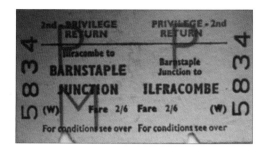

BARNSTAPLE JUNCTION

The demolition men have set to work and Barnstaple Junction B Box is now no more than a few small heaps of debris. Along with the box, the signals it controlled have also been removed, in the foreground can be seen the remains of a ground disc and signal recovered using the rail trolley, the end of which can just be seen on the siding adjacent to the former Ilfracombe line. The Nissen hut at top centre, recycled post WW2, is now a rare sight. Beyond the BMC ganger's lorry there is still plenty of activity across the yard, including a single rail-borne Ford Anglia. Latterly British Rail lost all interest in freight along the branch, just as they did with so many other West Country locations: trainloads of timber from Barnstaple Junction were no more attractive than trainloads of cars to Exmouth Junction - it was all just too much trouble.   (Tony Woodforth)

SR BARNSTAPLE to ILFRACOMBE

TAW BRIDGE, BARNSTAPLE

Left - The 08.05 Paddington – Ilfracombe, a Summer Saturdays only service of nine coaches, rumbles slowly over Barnstaple bridge drawn by a Hymek in 1968.

BARNSTAPLE TOWN

Right - The interior of Barnstaple Town signal box after closure, and before it was used by the Lynton &n Barnstaple revivalists as a museum. The windows have been smashed and even the oven doors have gone! Levers have been pulled, but no more holidaymakers will run past here on the rails. (July 1977)

Below - Looking back from the signalman's point of view towards the Taw Bridge in happier times. (Tony Woodforth) The Commercial Road signal box (**bottom right**) was burnt out shortly after the line closed, the intensity of the fire melting the lead off the roof.

Opposite, top right - As referred to on page 10, the bridge remained in situ in case the line reopened, but by 1977 all hope had gone and demolition was inevitable. (Tony Woodforth)

Opposite, bottom- During 1977 Industrial Dismantling (Steel and Plant Ltd) of Exeter have been hard at work, removing the Barnstaple Taw Bridge, although apparently with a small workforce! All the track, decking and support girders have gone and the bolts are being cut as work now progresses back towards Town station - just off view to the top left. (Tony Woodforth)

Braunton has been extensively covered in *In the Tracks of the 'ACE'* but this view of the B3231 (Caen Street) crossing was irresistible. The down road has been lifted, but everything else is still in place – even the 'To the National' buses' green and white enamel sign, still very common although the National Omnibus Company had been merged with the GWR and SR services to form Western and Southern National nearly forty years previously!   (Tony Woodforth)

Left - Braunton Gates guarded the crossing of Chapel Street, just to the south of the station whilst the 'keeper at Georgeham crossing **(right),** just to the north, was provided with a very handsome cottage..

14

MORTEHOE & WOOLACOMBE

Not looking much like a desirable holiday destination, DMU set 408 stands at Mortehoe & Woolacombe after labouring up the long and steep climb from Braunton. It is surrounded by a depressing scene of dereliction and decay, and the sea air has meant that the long neglected metalwork of the canopy and railings show more rust than paint. Perhaps the only highlight is the poster for Circus Hoffman (although the sticker might just indicate that it has been cancelled!). In spite of all this, a few determined passengers are still evident in this 1970 view.

Surprisingly, although it was still rotting in the early 1980s, by the middle of the decade it had been restored to a near-railway state and ex-BR Mk1 carriages can be seen here today. (Tony Woodforth)

Right - The heyday of the town as a resort may be drawing to a close, but the scale of much of the station facilities is easily seen. 'West Country' Pacific No. 34020 *Seaton* is ready to tackle the fearsome 1 in 36 gradient up to Mortehoe whilst the carriage sidings contain a set of Bulleid's comfortable post-war vehicles no doubt to form a Summer Saturday express to Waterloo later in the day. To the right is the goods shed with the engine shed and turntable behind the photographer. For a while in the early post-war period this was the destination of the Southern's celebrated 'Devon Belle' train with its Pullman Observation Car from which the delights of the North Devon countryside could be enjoyed in luxury.

Below - For decades, many of our seaside resorts had been served by regular coastal services, and paddle steamers such as the PS *Bristol Queen* would have taken trippers to Lundy Island or along the coast. The *Bristol Queen* was in service from 1946-68 with P & A Campbell Ltd, usually working out of Bristol, Cardiff and Ilfracombe, along with her sister *Cardiff Queen*. Campbell's, which originated with the famous Clyde Steamers in Glasgow, also owned the *Waverley*, which still plies its trade along the coast here during the summer. The *Bristol Queen* was withdrawn in 1967after damaging a paddle wheel and was broken up in Antwerp in March 1968.

Insets - After the Western Region had taken over the Southern lines in the West the through trains to Waterloo ceased and the carriage sidings became redundant. In the final years blue DMUs formed most of the trains, supplemented in high summer by through trains - ironically from Paddington - headed by 'Warships'. The carriage sidings were lifted between the announcement of closure in 1968 and closure in 1970.

Above - Without the glamour of a steam engine, station forecourts were often ignored by photographers. This scene shows at least 26 people and only three cars – a Ford Zephyr Mk 11, a Morris Minor 1000 and a Humber Super Snipe. Notice how the Zephyr sports a new sill in primer and the Humber has lost a sizeable area of wheel-arch and sill to the effects of sea air! Prior to arriving at an accommodation with the LSWR, the GWR had operated a horse drawn service using four horse-breaks, in competition with the railway. By the way, the shifty-looking man running past the Ford (indicated) hasn't stolen a handbag - there's a woman just behind him who is clutching it!

LYNTON & LYNMOUTH

The former Lynton & Barnstaple Railway station at Lynton survives as do others along the line, still looking much as they did when the last train left on 29 September 1935. Like its neighbour at Ilfracombe, the station suffered from having been built to boost local tourism, but was too far from the town. The innovative, early attempt to run a connecting bus motor bus service soon resulted in court action and the sale of the vehicles to the GWR, where they became No's 1+2 in that companies roadmotor fleet. The modern day L & B revival group plan eventually to divert to a new northern terminus near Valley of Rocks, a local beauty spot, and are aiming for a site at Blackmoor Gate to the south. .

For enthusiasts exploring backwaters of our rail system, finding long lost lines could be a challenge. Here at Spreycott though, the L & B could be explored from the comfort of a motor car as a section of the trackbed now forms a road. Just one more of the obstacles that the revivalists have to face. Elsewhere, bridges have been bypassed and neglected. In the shorter term, the Parracombe embankment which was washed away in the Lynmouth floods of 1952 requires replacement. Interestingly, the adjacent road embankment, built to bypass the village's steep, narrow road was constructed by Devon County Council using their contemporary portable narrow gauge railway system. This equipment included seven Kerr Stuart Wren locos which also saw use at Tavistock and Beacon Down Quarry only yards from the L & B at what is now Killington Lane Halt. These two industrial railway systems shared the same gauge but were not connected.

CHELFHAM VIADUCT

The 'Last Train' is seen on Chelfham Viaduct on 29 September 1935. The following day a wreath was left at Barnstaple Town station by Woody Bay resident Captain Thomas A Woolf RN (ret) with an inscription that included the prescient words 'Perchance it is not dead, but sleepeth'.

Many structures and parts of the trackbed remained and in 1994 the Lynton & Barnstaple Railway Trust was formed to purchase the trackbed of the historic line. The station at Woody Bay reopened in 2003 with newly-laid track for about half a mile to the south of the station. The replica L & B Manning Wardle loco, 'Lyd', *(below)* visited Woody Bay with ex-L&B coach No 15 and Observation car No 102 from the Festiniog Railway in September 2010 to celebrate the 75th Anniversary of the closure. The loco is seen running round at Woody Bay and carrying a replica of the wreath used in 1935.

WOODY BAY
reopened 11-5-2003

"I decided to visit this historic event by public transport, the journey to Barnstaple was quite an event, but nothing compared to the onward leg to Woody Bay. Having tendered my fare, the driver told me that he knew a bit about the line and several unscheduled stops were made as part of the running commentary provided by our very proud but unofficial tour guide!" A replica of the loco 'Lyn' is currently under construction as part of the plan to recreate an L & B train running from a new terminal at Lynton to Blackmoor Gate, and, eventually, back to Barnstaple.

L & B Observation Saloon Brake No 2 at Clannaborough Rectory near Bow. The forward thinking directors introduced eight observation coaches, originally with open ends, although the local climate soon caused the addition of glazing. Both nos. 1 & 2 acquired steam heating under Southern ownership - at 35' long, seating was provided for seventeen first and eight third class passengers plus guard. In spite of being some of the best rolling stock built for UK narrow gauge lines, by 29 September 1935 when the line closed there was little resale market and most vehicles were scrapped. The bodies having been burnt off, the underframes, along with three locomotives - all reduced to piles of scrap by John Cashmore - a foretaste of their close involvement in the wholesale destruction of redundant BR equipment in the 1960s.

Coach No2 was sold off for use as a summer house as seen here over thirty years later. By this time the "green" livery it carried was not the Maunsell shade it once carried. The vehicle is now preserved, but currently unrestored at the National Railway Museum.

In the early 1960s the underframe of a wagon used during the construction of the line was found and this has now returned to the L & B along with the remains of a covered van found more recently as a garden shed, both near Pilton. Leant against the coach is the enamel station nameboard from Blackmoor Gate. With the closure of the line came hardship for many of those associated with it; the driver of the last train found that his footplate experience was regarded as worthless to the Southern, whose only offer of alternative employment was as a labourer at Exmouth Junction Concrete Works. (Chris Tilley)

BARNSTAPLE JUNC TO BARNSTAPLE VICTORIA ROAD — closed 5-3-70

The connecting line from Victoria Road to the Junction station (**left**) across the River Taw (**below**) opened in June 1887, allowing the GWR to run services through to Ilfracombe. For most of its life this link was only used during the summer, but with the closure of Victoria Road to passengers on 12 June 1960 all passenger trains from Taunton were diverted to the Junction station.

№ 893
GREAT WESTERN RAILWAY.

TRAIN STAFF TICKET.

BARNSTAPLE.

Train No. _____ (DOWN.)

To the Engine-driver.
You are authorised, after seeing the Train Staff for the Section, to proceed from BARNSTAPLE SOUTH JUNCTION to BARNSTAPLE JUNCTION, SOUTHERN RLY., and the Train Staff will follow.
Signature of Person in Charge _____
Date _____

BARNSTAPLE VICTORIA ROAD

Nos. 41206 and 41291 are seen on the 'Exmoor Ranger' special train of 27 March 1965. Working from Exeter via Okehampton and Torrington, the locos have run round prior to departure for Ilfracombe, the last steam working over the branch. The single line working arrangements here were quite complex with signalboxes at Victoria Road, East Loop Junction and South Loop Junction as well as the Barnstaple Junction East signalbox (later, from 1949, 'A 'box) approaching the SR Junction station. For Ilfracombe trains the frequent token, staff and tablet exchanges continued at the West, or B, box, and then through Town station and Pottington, just beyond Barnstaple Town station.

Victoria Road from the cattle pens looking towards Taunton. After closure to passengers, the sizeable goods shed at Victoria Road remained in use until 5 March 1970 but now as an NCL railhead distribution depot for parcels and smalls traffic, as seen here. The wooden station buildings, which had become very dilapidated, stood where the 'Atkinson' lorry is parked on the left. The engine shed, also wooden, stood on the right of the row of vans which are parked on the connection to Junction station, by now just a long siding. Today the photographer would find himself in the middle of a road with the edge of the platform just visible. The former East and South Loop Signal Boxes have long gone, the site being covered by the sprawl of a supermarket. The goods shed has become a chapel but its origins are commemorated in a stained glass window. (Tony Woodforth)

SWIMBRIDGE

As a result of regional boundary changes in the early 1950s, Swimbridge has lost its dark and light stone paintwork in favour of Southern Region green and cream. Following rationalisatiion, the unusual signal box dating from the 1930s, was one of the last remaining in use. For westbound trains, there were two different key tokens used, for Victoria Road or the short section to East Loop Signal Box for through trains. On 20 August 1961 it was only the station staff await the arrival of a mogul hauled morning train for Taunton.

FILLEIGH

The photographer is leaning out of the window of a Barnstaple-bound train, but will need to duck back in quickly as a BR 82xxx-hauled Taunton train approaches. Being at the end of the platform the signal box gave a good view of the yard but it meant a long walk for the exchange of tokens, therefore, as at Dulverton, an auxiliary token instrument was provided. This signalbox closed and the station became unstaffed in September 1964.

Just beyond the double compound a line curves away behind the signal box to the goods shed and a short private siding to the Fortescue Estate warehouse. When the former alignment through the station was taken up by the North Devon Link Road, the associated earthworks were such that the last remnant of track, a buffer stop at the end of the Fortescue siding, was literally cut in half!
(both: Tony Woodforth)

Above - After closure the former station buildings at Filleigh became a private home with B & B accommodation and where fowl rule the roost. This was a far cry from the days when any potential new member of staff, having passed their railway interview had to be approved by Lady Acland before the job was confirmed, a situation that continued until at least WW2. Over the years the building has seen several alterations and extensions, the concrete hut being a standard product of the GWR Taunton Concrete Works. In front of this, the row of slabs mark the platform edge, with the trackbed and overbridge filled in by this April 1979 view. At the end of the ramp, the pedal car is a foretaste of what is to come, the site now being covered by the new A361 road.

Next page, top - Enjoying the fine weather of August 1963. Hanging out of the window of a Barnstaple train, No. 7333 would have provided a memorable moment with the smell a mix of smoke, steam and warm oil. Soon the engine would be opened up as it moved off the curving Filleigh Viaduct. The cost of repairs to this structure and the similar but shorter one at Venn Cross were given as the key elements to justify closure of the line. But the demolition men only took the iron spans and the piers remained. With the planned A361 North Devon Link Road using much of the old alignment from South Molton to Barnstaple, the piers were inspected and found to need nothing more than repointing before being fitted with a new concrete road deck twice the width of its predecessor!

SOUTH MOLTON

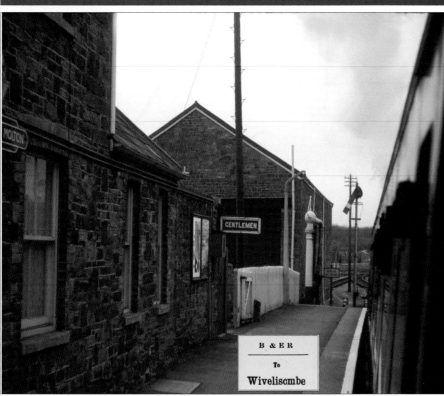

South Molton, along with Dulverton, was one of the busiest stations on the line. Evidently South Molton has had something of a makeover with new lamp posts and Totem signs, but the door still carries its GWR stone paint. Inside, the waiting room furniture harked back to an even earlier era, the table and chairs all clearly displaying their Bristol & Exeter Railway origins. Many of the stations were known for their racks of B & E luggage labels still stocked in the 1960s. Opening in 1873, the GWR took over operation when they absorbed the B & E in August 1876. In the line's heyday rabbit specials ran, through trains added and detached restaurant cars and even the Beatles on their Magical Mystery Tour tried to lunch on their special train here. It certainly wasn't No. D6336 that the local girls bunked off school to see! More recently, attempts were made to have the untouched former station given some protection by listing but, sadly, the building disappeared very quickly. Today only the former goods shed and part of the platform railings mark the location for passing motorists. 27 April 1963. (NH Pratt, col. Amyas Crump)

FLORENCE MINE TRAMWAY

Extensive ironstone mining operations were carried out around North Molton and a connecting tramway of 2' 6" gauge opened in 1874. Mining was intermittent and had ceased by 1900 but much of the alignment remains, as seen here with the sleeper marks still visible on the approach to the GWR transfer siding a short distance ahead.

EAST ANSTEY

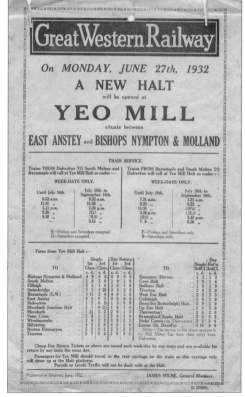

At 700' above sea level, East Ansty was the highest point on this forty two mile line. Goods facilities, withdrawn in September 1963, had been little used for many years, one of the sidings being given over to a camping coach whose incumbents were unlikely to be much disturbed by the monthly market. East Anstey was also responsible for Yeo Mill Halt just over a mile further west. (J Bennett, col. Amyas Crump)

DULVERTON

As its name suggests, the Devon & Somerset Railway crossed parts of both counties. For a few miles around Dulverton the line was in Somerset, as it was again from Venn Cross to Norton Fitzwarren: it has been included here as it was the junction for Exe Valley services. In this delightful shot taken in July 1962, No. 1442 on the Exe Valley auto is, unusually, in the up platform. Having not long been repainted, the station and its many ancillary buildings look very smart. A Porter has a barrow load of parcels - perhaps the reason for the platform change. Further along the platform, the barrow fitted with a support bar and tarpaulin was peculiar to this station, but the slate hung building confirms the need for protection from Exmoor weather. As with so many locations, the signalman at Morebath Junction would rely on cans of water being supplied from the nearest convenient station. The empty can has been left on the platform by a passing Barnstaple train.

DULVERTON

Above - Demonstrating the need for weather protection here, the auto at its normal platform, has drawn forward for water in pouring rain! Unusually, the supply tank for the station was set into the ground behind the front of the coach which on this occasion is one of the two named trailers, 'Thrush'. At the base of the signal, the small hut held the auxiliary token instrument, the same arrangement as applied at Filleigh. In the days before auto working was introduced, and for freight trains, engines were turned on a small turntable in the yard. Or, as happened on at least one occasion, they ended up in the pit and required assistance from the Exeter breakdown gang. Even in the 1950s Service Time Tables there was reference to tender engines not being used 'until a large turntable is provided at Dulverton'.

Right - No. 3205 with its colourful mix of stock, is working the Ilfracombe - Exeter via Taunton leg of the Exmoor Ranger on 27 March 1965. To the right sidings have been lifted and the Exe Valley rails are rusty. With the demise of interchange and freight traffic, the station became little more than a halt towards the end. The signalbox was one of several destined to close before the line itself so making for some lengthy block sections. The well endowed telegraph pole carries the railway's own internal circuits for the lines to Barnstaple, Exeter and Taunton. For No. 3205, withdrawal but then preservation was the plan when the train got back to Exeter. But as happened so often, internal communication was such that within days the engine had been reallocated to Templecombe and preservation had to wait.

In the Summer 1963, No. 6327 is departing on a Taunton train made up of ex-mainline Collett and Hawkesworth stock. The loco had moved west from Swindon to work out its last year prior to being withdrawn from Taunton in September 1963, one of the last places where the Moguls had worked. The white lineside equipment to the left of the second coach is one of the rarely photographed automatic token exchangers. The design of these was based on the Whitaker apparatus used on the Somerset & Dorset line. A number of Taunton allocated engines used on the Minehead and Barnstaple branches had their bunkers or tenders fitted with the matching pick-up/set-down jaw on an extending arm to permit exchanges at up to 40 mph. These were installed as part of improvements undertaken in the 1930s to speed up services on these two lines.

"In the last days of the line my parents visited Dulverton regularly, but the only time I saw a train was a single car diesel unit near Wiveliscombe. It was not long before I saw the demolition team at work hauling the last remains of the centre span from the picturesque River Exe bridge along the empty trackbed back to Dulverton. Somehow this inspired me to persuade a friend to join me for a cycle ride to Milverton and then along the ballast to Wiveliscombe. The obvious problems of trying to cycle over loose ballast were soon compounded by the discovery of a vital bridge having been removed in the week since our last visit. My failure to think of taking a puncture repair kit was matched only by the frustration of not having a camera." Today the goods shed and station buildings remain as private houses, although the canopy and wall hanging slates have long gone. (J Bennett, col. Amyas Crump)

MOREBATH

By August 1963 the passing loop at Morebath was out of use and all signal arms had been removed. The signal box, closed on 2 March, would soon disappear along with the remains of its equipment. No. 7333 is running along the remaining single line, formerly the down loop. The goods shed too had closed two months previously, together with its load gauge both now 'redundant assets'. The local permanent way gang have the largest hut on the line!

In 1969, with windows open and all the glass broken, it would require some imagination to see that here was a solidly built structure on a large plot which would make a good home.
(J Bennett, col. Amyas Crump)

OUR LOCAL EXPRESS   TAUNTON to BARNSTAPLE

Left top and bottom - Rusted rails in the goods yard are testament that Venn Cross is nearing the end of its glory days. Churchward Mogul No. 6372 on a westbound passenger train passes a goods which has evidently no traffic for Venn Cross.

Above - Redundant station steps at Wiveliscombe.

I wonder who might have asked Father Christmas for a train set? Bampton C.1949. (Tiverton Museum)

Pages 39 to 41 - The once picturesque station at Bampton on the Tiverton & North Devon Railway, part of the Exe Valley branch south of Morebath Junction, now plays host only to the demolition team from Pittrail Ltd whose caravan is on the platform. All of the down line and the rails of the up line have gone. In the yard (overleaf) work is ongoing, but soon it will be time to move on. Unusually, Bampton's picturesque station was very close to the town centre and ideally placed as a railhead to the surrounding agricultural communities. In the Edwardian era, the station gardens were impressive enough to justify a series of postcards being published, just one aspect of its colourful history so easily forgotten as being from a forgotten age. Another memory was to the South of the town, where there was considerable opposition from a local landowner when the line was being promoted. As work started on his land, the fight continued with gangs of men being employed at night to undo that which the railway navvies had built during the day! Eventually order had to be established and construction continued.

Demolition day at Bampton.

Cove Signal Box, viewed from a passing car post closure in 1964, shews weeds growing in the track, but the lamp is still on the level crossing gate - but which would now no longer entertain local children with a ride as it was opened and closed. There were four other similar crossings on the Exe Valley line. A siding was provided to the North for a nearby quarry but saw little traffic; the quarry Foreman was required to apply to the Crossing Keeper for permission to blast and to check that the line was clear afterwards. The signalman's cottage and the signalbox itself remain today, converted into comfortable living accommodation as with so many 'surplus' railway properties.

Immediately to the South of the crossing was Cove Halt whose pagoda shelter today does service at Donniford on the West Somerset Railway. For trains running downhill to Tiverton, the crew would soon be taking a liberal view of the overall speed restriction on the line of just 35mph. It was almost a point of honour that the one mile straight leading to Bolham Halt would be covered in one minute.

SPOTLIGHT TIVERTON

In each volume we focus on one particularly fascinating location.

For this Devon volume we feature the lines which connected at TIVERTON, and the CULM VALLEY branch line to HEMYOCK.

"An outing with fellow members of the Great Western Society provided my first experience of 'Impermanent Ways' this on a visit to Tiverton's derelict station. With all the doors open or hanging off, it was an eerie experience to stand in a room littered with broken glass and shattered woodwork, at the same time being shewn (the GWR's preferred spelling!) pictures of the station in all its former glory. The yard occupied a considerable area and with the track only recently lifted, the impressions of many hundreds of sleepers left a lasting impression of the sadness and waste of the railway in its rationalised and 'modern' era. In a time when distance and personal contact are of little consequence, it still amazes me that the GWR, and SR, put so much importance on maintaining close connections with the communities they served - it was the responsibility of every member of staff to seek out new opportunities.

"Many years later I was to discover firsthand that a trainload of freight a day to Tiverton was a nuisance to the railway - because the last two miles of the journey were rather inconvenient. The extraordinary effort that went in to proving that closure was the only

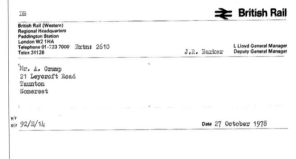

British Rail

DB

British Rail (Western)
Regional Headquarters
Paddington Station
London W2 1HA
Telephone 01-723 7000   Extns 2610
Telex 24126

J.R. Barker

L Lloyd General Manager
Deputy General Manager

Mr. A. Crump
21 Leycroft Road
Taunton
Somerset

y/r
o/r 92/E/14   Date 27 October 1978

Dear Sir

APPLICATION TO PURCHASE STATION SIGNS TIVERTON JUNCTION

Thank you for your letter of 6 October. The station signs you refer to are available for disposal and are priced as below, plus V.A.T. :-

Signal box cast iron nameplate -	£40.00
Totem station signs - two each -	£35.00
Wooden hanging sign "Waiting Room" -	£ 7.50
Wooden hanging sign "Ladies" -	£ 7.50
Wooden hanging sign "Gentlemen" - two each -	£ 2.50 each
Wooden station board -	£ 2.50

If you wish to avail yourself of this offer, kindly forward the total purchase amount to me and I will arrange for a letter of authority to be issued.

Conditions of sale are :-

(a) The items are removed and transported by the purchaser at a time convenient to the Supervisor responsible for the area, to ensure that security and regulations are observed.

(b) Clearance from the site has to be made at your own expense, without assistance from British Rail Staff.

(c) British Railways Board shall in no way be liable for injury, damage or loss, which may be incurred by you, your agent, persons or property, whilst on British Rail property for the purpose of removing the signs.

Please advise me by 17 November whether you wish to proceed with this purchase.

Yours faithfully

for Stores Controller

BR 2001/96

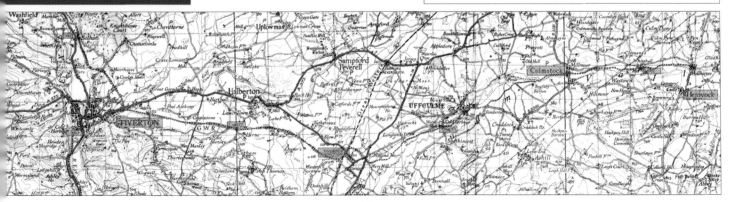

option for an unwanted, but viable part of the system, is a story often told but still represents one of the greatest scandals of modern times. In the case of Tiverton, the loss of the railway has changed the focus of the communities of the Exe Valley, much of the local commerce centred solely around the M5 motorway corridor.

TIVERTON   closed (p) 5-10-64 (g) 5-6-67

"In consequence the town centre is now empty the shops are closing, and, as yet, the town still has not been able to fully develop its tourist industry. Much of this era of social change is represented in the award-winning Tiverton Museum of Mid Devon Rural Life, where ex Tivvy Bumper loco No. 1442 is by far the most popular exhibit for young and old visitors. Here it is surrounded by a wonderful collection of local railwayana representing something of the transport hub that the town was for people of the Culm and Exe Valleys."

Right - No. D6343 brings the last six coach up train into the station on 5 October 1963. The 22.05 Exeter to Bampton was running late as older members of the public look on, doubtless their minds filled with memories of a lifetime using the train. Others stand around, already disconnected. A Porter approaches apparently oblivious to all, he would still have a job on Monday as the 'Bumper' would still be running. Exeter Shed was by now short of suitable steam power to work the train, six coaches too much for a 14xx. There were still ex Great Western 57xx panniers at Exmouth Junction which would have been ideal, but old rivalries died hard. (Peter Gray)

44

TIVERTON

Following the demise of the Exe Valley, the 'Tivvy Bumper' connection to Tiverton Junction remained until 5 October 1964 and freight - usually worked by a D63xx - until 5 June 1967. To keep passengers dry during inclement weather and give them a shorter walk, the Bumper was diverted into the former down platform where No. 1450 is seen just before closure. Passenger workings on the Bumper and Culm Valley were never dieselised, with few diesel workings on the Exe Valley line. The Culm Valley branch had its own special limitations, but when diesel requirements were assessed, no provision was made, because the decision to do away with the services had been made years before the public were informed. Hauled by No. 1450, the last Bumper consisted of trailers W225/8W, both now on the South Devon Railway. (John Phillips, col. Amyas Crump)

TIVERTON

The fine old market town of Tiverton gained much wealth in the heyday of the woollen industry, a subsequent decline being arrested when Heathcoat's set up their well known lace factory. With a population approaching 10,000 at the opening of the Bristol & Exeter Railway, a direct connection to that system was felt to be vital for continuing prosperity. The broad gauge branch opened four years later in 1848, to a terminus adjacent to what had been London Road (now Blundells Road). Within the fertile Exe Valley, there were calls for better communication with both Tiverton and Exeter, but with money short progress was slow. Eventually, with GWR support and a revised route (the Bolham Deviation), the through line was completed from Stoke Canon Junction to Morebath Junction in 1885, using a new site for the through station and its associated service to Tiverton Junction. This, like the Culm Valley Branch (opened 1876), was standard gauge by which time the main line had been converted to mixed gauge from Taunton to Exeter in anticipation of the new traffic.

The site of Tiverton's old terminus became part of the enlarged goods yard and today the Brunelian goods shed with its later additions still forms an obvious landmark. West Exe Halt (see page 50) opened in March 1928, mainly to serve the nearby Heathcoat's factory: it also marked the point at which the original route to Bolham was intended to diverge and go in a sweeping curve around the West side of the town, before turning North on a similar line to that actually used, but at a different level. *(For further details please see The Tiverton Museum Railway Collection).*

THE TIVERTON MUSEUM
RAILWAY COLLECTION

Compiled by Amyas Crump

TIVERTON

The now derelict station just before final demolition and seen as it did the only time I ever saw it, on 5 July 1970. Looking north, in the distance can just be seen the houses along Old Blundells Road near to the former gasworks. At the southern end of the station, Canal Road bridge has since been replaced with a roundabout. The trackbed, left untouched for years until the new relief road was built, was much used by locals as a popular walk. The extensive facilities of this once very busy station were well built and following demolition much of the material was sold off. Most of the stone went to a builder at Blue Anchor but there are several examples around Tiverton where part has been used for building or decorative purposes. (Bert Demelweek, col. Amyas Crump)

The Tiverton station frontage. At the time of opening the facilities provided were: First Class Waiting Room, First and Second Class Ladies Waiting Room, Third Class Ladies Waiting Room, General Waiting Rooms, Booking Office and Station Master. Beyond the entrance/exit were the Parcels & Cloak Rooms, Urinals, Lamp and Porters Rooms. (See also the 'under the canopy' image on page 44 with its characteristic hanging and information signs.) For many a closed Great Western station, the last remaining landmark has been the Scots Pine trees so often planted by the GWR from their nurseries, one of the last of these being at Taunton. Tiverton, unusually, had its approach road lined by an avenue of Lime trees. Perhaps equally unusually, the town centre was only a few minutes walk away, contributing to the substantial volumes of traffic handled here. (Sean Bolan)

The Exe Valley and its associated services provided some of the last regular work for the 14xx class. No. 1442 had been made redundant from Oxford by dieselisation and moved to Exeter to replace other older, more worn members of the class for the last year of service. After the branch closure No. 1442, along with No. 1450, was temporarily used on the Yeovil Town - Junction and Seaton Branch trains before being finally withdrawn in May 1965. As one of the last survivors No. 1442 was bought by Lord Amory and presented to the town museum. Following restoration at Swindon, the engine worked a special train from Tiverton Junction to the site of the original Tiverton Station where the BR crew took their leave and returned to Exmouth Junction shed by road Royal Engineers assisted with the move to a plinth in adjacent Blundells Road where weather gradually took its toll. To prevent further deterioration No. 1442 has been provided with a special gallery in the Museum where she is surrounded by relics of the local rail network and is still much loved by the community.

GWR *EXE VALLEY* Railway   *closed 7-10-63*

WEST EXE HALT

All signs of the former halt which closed with the rest of the line in October 1963 have gone and the embankment lies bare. Soon it too will go, along with some cottages in the centre of this view, to make way for the town's new inner relief road. Less than half a mile away is the well known lace factory of John Heathcoat, the major employer locally. The halt carried considerable commuter traffic as a result. The factory also provided a considerable volume of parcels and freight traffic to the main station whose death knell was sounded when this traffic went to road haulage.   (Peter Triggs, col. Amyas Crump)

Just north of Cadeleigh station the line crossed the River which gave it its name. The line from Stoke Canon, on the Bristol & Exeter main line, to Tiverton was built by the GWR as the Exe Valley Railway, but together with the Tiverton & North Devon it was worked as one to form a single route connecting Exeter to the Devon & Somerset at Morebath Jct. One of several substantial similar structures along the line, only this bridge at Bickleigh remains, as it also carries mains utility services. Perhaps one day this

section of the trackbed may join Devon's increasing network of cycleways, but the return of trains is unlikely. Bickleigh's other nearby (road) bridge over the River Exe has long been regarded by locals as the inspiration for the iconic 1970 hit record 'Bridge Over Troubled Water' who remember Simon & Garfunkel playing locally. When in flood, the river is certainly dramatic, but elsewhere others have also claimed to have been the inspiration for the duo. (Chris Henley, col. Amyas Crump) **Left -** Further along, just north of Thorverton, a 14xx ambled along the Exe Valley in time-honoured fashion over a similar bridge, reminding us of what we have lost forever.

Cadeleigh near the end; the compact layout and picturesque charm of this station has inspired many a modeller. Beyond the station offices is the station master's house, with a glimpse of the bridge beyond. Opposite, the small wooden shelter and signalbox with matching valences have gone but may one day rise again. Serving a small community and a widespread agricultural area, this was rarely a busy place, and was originally named 'Cadeleigh and Bickleigh' - it was actually situated in the latter village, Cadeleigh being some 1½ miles distant. Before the coming of the railway, the road ran straight across the foreground, as it does again today. "Bickleigh proved a very expensive place" said the Engineer when building the line, It is a place of bridges, the photographer standing on one of the many required to deal with rail, road and stream.

Following track clearance the station area was used by Devon County Council for open storage, the buildings remaining largely untouched. For a time it was the focal point for the aspirations of the *Mid Devon Tramway Preservation Society* whose aim was to lay about one and a half miles of line from a Park and Ride facility with the old station as the central point. Eventually the site was disposed of in Spring 1997 to become the Devon Railway Centre and marketed as "The Station that Time Forgot". (Chris Henley, col. Amyas Crump)

Aside from the standard gauge exhibition train, there is now an extensive collection of narrow gauge material including a very early wheelset found under a bush in Tiverton! The slate wagon in the foreground was built by the GWR for use at Blaenau Ffestiniog; it has since been sold to the Great Western Society at Didcot, fulfilling a long held wish to exhibit broad, standard and narrow gauge rolling stock. Appropriately, there have also been visits by preserved ex DCC Highways steam locos, *Peter Pan* and *Pixie*.

Probably a unique image of the day Thorverton played host to the passage of the down Torbay Express on 1 October 1960 when flooding had caused closure of the WR main line around Hele & Bradninch, trains being diverted via Tiverton and the Exe Valley line to Stoke Canon. A neighbour heard this labouring locomotive approach with its heavy train and was just in time to snatch a photo. During the afternoon a number of through trains were diverted this way before the line Tiverton also became flooded. Over the years there had been a number of such diversions, and during WW2 the signal boxes were staffed continuously, especially useful on occasions such as that when the main line was blocked by the Norton Fitzwarren crash of 1940. (David Massey, col. Amyas Crump)

Tender engines were rare on the Exe Valley, classified as a yellow availability route. Instructions in the General Appendix to the Rule Book detailed how larger engines than the normal 14 xx / 57xx might could be used, tender engines having to be placed in front of tanks when double heading. As far as is known the Royal Train first visited Thorverton c1930 for the distribution of Maunday Money. On 2/3 July 1952 the train was brought here from Newton Abbot by Manor class Nos. 7801 'Anthony Manor' and 7806 'Cockington Manor'. In 1961 Mogul No. 7337 has brought the train, working wrong line, into the platform where the Duke of Edinburgh transferred to the Westland helicopter which is just departing. This record of the event was taken from the Station Master's bedroom window. (Suzanne Massey, col. Amyas Crump)

THORVERTON

The late afternoon sun shines on Thorverton in June 1962 as a northbound train waits to cross an Exeter working. Taken from the entrance to the goods yard, which by this time saw little more than the odd coal wagon and withdrawn stock for storage, non wagonload traffic had long been rationalised as a result of the Great Western 'Zonal' Freight Collection and Delivery scheme. The empty sidings had once provided an idyllic location for a camping coach.

Leaning against the wall is the ganger's trolley and behind it, the fence is in need of paint. Work had in fact started and got as far as the end loading dock gates, as seen here, that is before the men were withdrawn, never to return.
(John Phillips, col. Amyas Crump)

Last ticket issued. The last train on a Saturday usually worked back to Exeter via Tiverton Junction. On the main line the little 14xxs were well able to take advantage of the opportunity for speed presented by the main line - a journey which with the trailer leading would undoubtedly have been exhilarating! On the last day the service worked back down the branch stopping at all stations, arriving here at nearly midnight. For the sale of this the last ticket issued, Station Master Reg Coles noted that it had just passed midnight and thus he changed the date on the ticket stamping press - consequently this last ticket carries a date of issue for the day after closure!

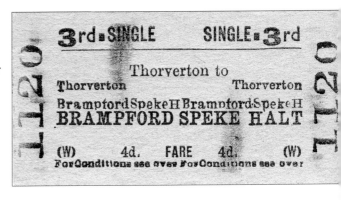

With branch line closures prominent in the news, a campaign was started locally under the banner 'Exe Valley Enterprise' which purpose was to encourage use of the trains, protests being regarded as useless. To further promote the 'other useful services at your helpful local station' in spite of British Railways, two Saturday evening First Class only excursions were run from Dulverton to Exeter Central and Exmouth in Spring 1962, with others planned. Schemes were put forward to retain a route from Tiverton Junction via Tiverton, Bampton and Dulverton to Barnstaple intended to keep the principle towns of the area rail connected. But the likes of Stanley Raymond at Paddington and the British Railways Board were not to be moved. Who would have foreseen that petrol would rise in price to the current level of over six pounds a gallon!

After closure to passengers, freight continued to run to Thorverton Mill where the former BSA motorcycle-engined wagon pusher had been replaced by a Fordson tractor within the private siding. This too ended, on 30 November 1966. After track lifting the underbridge was removed and the station site sold. Sadly the signalbox became firewood, but the station was extended with material from the goods shed and became known as 'Beechings Way'.

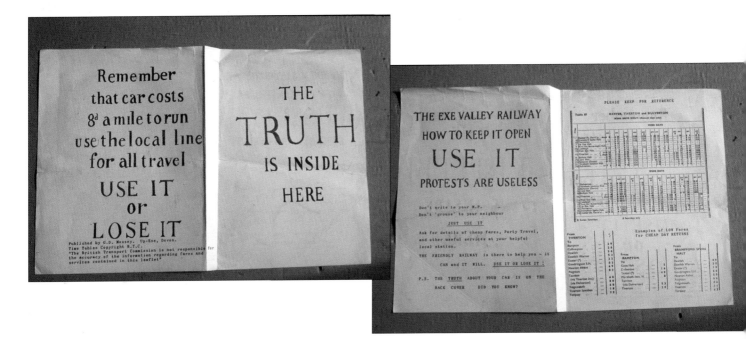

GWR *TIVERTON to TIVERTON JUNCTION*

closed 5-10-67

HALBERTON HALT
closed 5-10-64

Left and below - In this view through the Driver's vestibule of the auto-coach, the Tivvy Bumper pulls briskly away from the single coach length platform of Halberton Halt, the only intermediate stopping place on this line, opened on 5 December 1927. The double track width of the over bridge affording additional shelter. In the foreground is the top of the handbrake and hanging from its bracket above the centre window, is the regulator handle. Outside, the tail lamp shows signs of age. The halt displays some of the usual collection of bicycles which were safely left unlocked here day after day. (Peter Triggs, col. Amyas Crump)

Having been built for a double line of broad gauge rails (7' 0¼"), but only having had a single track laid, there was plenty of space after conversion to standard gauge (which took place in June 1884) to provide a connection to the Tiverton & North Devon Branch. From the late 1920s this stretch of line had a most unusual landmark in the form of an apple orchard two miles long and one tree wide along the spare formation. With closure came the sale of land and now the halt and its orchard are but a memory.

The steam from the safety valves of the 'Hall' standing with a northbound train partially obscures the rails of the Hemyock branch as it curves away from the down side. Meanwhile a 14xx takes water in the Tiverton branch platform. Motive power for both the Tiverton and Hemyock branches was provided from Exeter, the normal allocation being two members of the 14xx type, one for each branch. Closure of the line from Tiverton came on 5 October 1964, the remaining local freight services initially worked by 204hp diesel shunters from Exeter. These were soon replaced by the more suitable, but even less reliable North British D63xx, No. D6339 the last in service when it worked a trip to Hemyock on 1 January 1972, the day after those still in use had been officially withdrawn.

The Tiverton Branch trailed in to the up side of the station, where there was also a covered platform for butter and parcels traffic. The Culm Valley branch, having dropped down the 1 in 67 from Crossways cutting, which often defeated the diminutive early engines, trailed in to the down side. During the last week of service prior to closure on 7 September 1963, No. 1450 and a mixed train cast a shadow over the platform as they prepare to depart for Hemyock. Apparently the slowest train service on British Railways and the last place one might travel in gas lit carriages, this really was the end of an era! No. 1450 is still with us today and has been enjoyed on a number of ex-GWR branch lines, often paired with an auto-trailer. Perhaps her moment of glory is still to come as the engine is booked to appear in a remake of 'The Titfield Thunderbolt'. Alongside the venerable iron mink has lost its running gear to become an additional secure store in this busy yard.

Right - The wrecked interior of the 1932 built signal box is seen following the introduction of the Exeter MAS scheme. There is little left to show for the decades of care lavished by generations of signalmen, all the instruments, their shelf and most of the 120 levers have gone. Of the many spaces in this frame, two can be accounted for by having been presented to Tiverton Museum. Lever 111 still bears its wartime scars, having had a bullet lodged in the top of the handle when a Home Guard rifle was accidentally fired during a late night patrol visit. There were very few facilities for warmth and a cuppa in rural areas during wartime.

Left - The right hand span of the footbridge has gone and all the butter platform with its associated buildings have also been cleared in this July 1988 view. The down platform shows that closed lines and stations can provide rich pickings for railway revivalists. The lamp posts having gone to the West Somerset Railway for station restoration while the slabs went to the Great Western Society. GWS members lifted the slabs which were then loaded in to rail wagons stabled on the old Culm Valley line for onward transmission to Didcot where they have been reused. This siding was also used in a short lived project to convey traffic from Redlands tile works at Westleigh.

Right - A very clean class 47 heads west To the left is the oil storage depot provided for Chivenor airfield. Curving to the right are the stark remains of the Culm Valley branch lifted only a few months before its centenary. Above the truncated branch, the M5 has a distinctive hump, a result of the hundreds of thousands of pounds spent on engineering it to bridge the railway which then closed as the motorway was being built. A short stretch of track was lifted to enable the motorway works to continue without construction of the intended bridge. In the vee between the branch and down loop had once been a siding to enable gravity run round before the station was extended and facilities improved circa 1932.

GWR CULM VALLEY branch

COLDHARBOUR HALT

Left - A siding had been laid here at Coldharbour shortly after the branch opened in 1876 to serve the adjacent woollen mill. The halt came much later, opening on 23 February 1929. When the passenger service ended the Crossing Keeper's hut and nameboard found further use in a local garden. The nameboard, along with all the others from the branch, was eventually recovered for display with No. 1442 and other local relics in Tiverton. Having closed commercially, the mill is now run by enthusiasts, visitors parking here on the site of the railway.

UFFCULME

Right - Looking across the base of the cattle pens at Uffculme towards Culmstock and Hemyock, the stop sign for the level crossing stands guard over an empty trackbed and the overgrown platform. George Small had operated a coal and agricultural feed business from here but by this time the Thomas Ward demolition crew had passed the coal yard, which was to the right, had gone. Soon the whole area would be cleared for housing. As at Bickleigh, there had been a short lived plan for The Mid Devon Tramway to build a museum on the station site and run a connecting service to Coldharbour Mill. As these notes are being written, there is a rather animated public meeting being held to discuss building a Culm Valley footpath / cycleway, largely on the old railway alignment. Doubtless, many of the arguments sounded will be very similar to those heard nearly one hundred and forty years earlier when the Light Railway was being promoted! (Both:Peter Triggs, col. Amyas Crump)

With the demise of passenger services in the Culm and Exe Valleys, Exeter's allocation of 14xx was withdrawn or moved away. By 1964 two of the last survivors were Nos. 1442 and 1450 which came back to Exeter (Exmouth Junction) to provide temporary cover for services at Yeovil and Seaton. Arrangements were made for No. 1450 to cover the Hemyock milk trip on 23 August 1964 and a Drivers' tea break at Tiverton Junction allowed the four photographers time for a start to be made on cleaning the loco. Both mechanically and externally it was by now very rundown and there was only time to clean the side that would be in the sun! Photo stops were made en route, here No. 1450 pulls across the crossing at the overgrown platform of Whitehall Halt. Siding traffic from the adjacent mill and the crossing keeper are long gone but newspapers continued to be distributed locally from a box on the site of the waiting shelter for many years after the end of passenger trains.

On the same day Hemyock presents a scene of rural charm as No. 1450 prepares to leave for the return journey. Behind the Austin A40 the railway has lost the coal traffic it once carried to the Creamery boiler house although oil traffic was still railborne at this time. In its early years the branch had played host to several lightweight non standard engines. To enable their replacement by standard 0-4-2 tanks the line had to be lowered through Crossways cutting (leaving Tiverton Junction) and bridges replaced. The stations were remodelled and, in the case of Hemyock, the goods, carriage and engine sheds were removed. The 1874-built timber engine shed was sold off for further use c1930 but still survived locally eighty years later. A smaller corrugated iron store for goods was provided (located to the right of this picture) and this too has survived the line it once served.
(Both: Chris Gammell, col. Amyas Crump)

WHITEHALL HALT

HEMYOCK

The empty platform is very different to how it was on 7 September 1963, for my sixth birthday outing when we went to see off the last train. In those days such events were attended in one's Sunday best which was usually school uniform. The narrow platform was crowded and I stood near the side gate clutching my ticket. The building continued to be staffed to administer the milk traffic. To the end of its life the Booking Office still held ledgers and records going back almost to the opening of the line. Another regular job was the upkeep and replenishment of the many crossing gate lamps. For the last months of the milk service, the buildings were demolished following complaints from train crews about sighting difficulties during shunting, something that had not seemed to bother steam crews for decades beforehand. A replacement office was provided in the form of a BR standard brake van with the addition of a telephone. (John Phillips, col. Amyas Crump)

SEATON JUNCTION

Above - This is one of the handful of places that I ever saw steam on BR in the form of a Bulleid Pacific at speed, although nameless No. 34099 (once 'Lynmouth') is here heading home to Salisbury with a stopper. Soon the WR took over **(right)** in the shape of hydraulics such as Hymek No. D7039, still in two tone green livery. Just visible in the down loop a DMU forms an Exeter stopping service, which would be withdrawn on 7 March 1966. Across the platform to the left, the branch train departed. The Civil Engineers Dept have work to do on the platform, but with no sign of activity, perhaps tea is being drunk elsewhere. In the yard stands an immaculate Express Dairy AEC lorry across the road from the Shute Arms Hotel. And there is of course that magnificent signal with its co-acting arms. (**above** - Bruce Oliver, **right** - col. Chris Henley)

The station closed along with the closure of the branch and cessation of main line stopping trains on 6 March 1966. General freight went shortly afterwards although coal and milk surviving a while longer (milk traffic ceased in early 1978). The signalbox and all buildings have gone from the branch platform, the station offices survive having seen a variety of commercial uses. Coal traffic for P R Hutchings was transferred to the newly opened Coal Concentration Depots at Taunton and Exmouth Junction for onward delivery by road, the extra handling being no help to a declining coal industry. The dairy was replaced by a new, road only, facility at Honiton. Likewise, the Shute Arms Hotel has long since closed its doors to staying guests. The singling of the former SR main line to Exeter has proved to be as short sighted as it was predicted to be, the most recent upgrade being the lengthy and costly loop at Axminster.
(col. Chris Henley)

COLYTON

South of Colyton in July 1962, M7 No. 30125 is propelling its train of Maunsell pull-push coaches towards Seaton past the water meadows of the River Coly. In this view, grass on the embankment sides has recently been burned (a spark from an engine perhaps or controlled bunring by the p/way gang?) and the boundary fence repaired. In the distance the historic town is expanding out along the road to Colyford. The branch services had been operated with former LSWR M7s for years, but from May 1963 onwards, and as a result of boundary changes which saw the Western taking over all lines west of Salisbury, these were replaced by Western Region 64xx pannier tanks. With steam in decline DMUs took over in November 1963 only to be ousted by steam for a final fling in February 1965. This was in the form of auto-trains hauled by ex GWR Nos. 1442 / 50 by now redundant from Tiverton and Hemyock. (Chris Gammell, col. Amyas Crump)

COLYTON

As a collector of old film, it can be interesting to revisit the spot where a particular shot was taken, as happened here. The intervening forty-six years have allowed considerable growth in all directions. It would appear that the then land owner was a very keen photographer and may well have invited Chris Gammell to use this hillside vantage spot back in 1962. Fifty years on from the view opposite, it is trams and not trains that rumble over the bridge, still with its original beams, cast by Kerslakes Foundry in Exeter.

SEATON

RAIL REPLACEMENT SERVICES

Previous page, lower - Seaton Station is seen in July 1960 from across the River Axe and where the Seaton & Beer Railway Co. built a concrete bridge and toll house opened in 1877 **(above)**.

Now a scheduled ancient monument as the 'oldest standing concrete bridge in England' it had to be sold off before the LSWR would buy the line. M7 No. 30048 with its two coach pull-push set is just leaving with a mid week service to the Junction. At this time the branch set consisted of one of the very recently converted Maunsell composite brake / open second pairings first introduced only the previous October. Spare coaches await their next duty - perhaps the following Saturday or perhaps earlier - for it is all too easy to forget that vast numbers of weekday and evening excursions still operated across the railway system at that time.

The railway embankment gave a fine view of the estuary and the tramway company now capitalises on this in a way that the railway never did. Kingfishers nest in the reeds along the Axe estuary and are a popular draw for 'Twitchers' as well as holidaymakers. Beyond the station was the gas works and a holiday camp which after much protest has been replaced by the ubiquitous supermarket.

Above right - One of the conditions imposed to allow closure of most lines was the provision of a replacement bus service. Southern and Western National buses owed their existence to the former Southern and Great Western Railways' road motor interests and continued the former railway practice of delivering parcels en route. In the mid 1970s as a ' junior' at work, I often took small parcels to Taunton Bus Station for delivery, the customers meeting the bus at their nearest stops, the routes to Glastonbur,y and Seaton via Chard being the most popular. All very cheap, quick and easy compared to the current practice of putting yet another vehicle on the road.

Seen at Seaton Bus Station Bristol LS (1778) TUO 494, dating from 1956 displays a suitably period destination 'Seaton (station)' this nearly a decade after the station had closed. Southern National vehicles were taken over by Western National in November 1969, No. 1778 survived in service for twenty years before being sold off in February 1977. The station itself was very close to the sea front, the Southern providing new art-deco style station facilities in concrete during the 1930s. Though regarded as very stylish, they were far from comfortable to work in once the balmy days of summer had passed. Enveloped in sea mist or with a wind blowing off the sea, conditions could be bleak. During wartime the Booking Office Clerk was replaced by a young lady, who with little or no heating and unable to wear gloves, was often in tears with the cold. It was reported as fortunate that one of the branch enginemen was able to provide some distraction.

SR SIDMOUTH & BUDLEIGH branches

Left - At Sidmouth Junc a filthy No. 34071 *601 Squadron* is arriving with a mid week train for Exeter in May 1964 - the last summer of steam working on the line. The waiting passengers will be pleased to see that the stock is rather cleaner, hopefully the passengers for the up train signalled will be similarly treated. Over in the yard sits something of a mystery (inset below), but perhaps an interesting prototype for modellers, in the form of a narrow gauge coach. Having been unable to find anything definite of its history, any information would be welcome. Two similar bodies existed for many years in a field near here, at Venn Ottery near Tipton St Johns.

Right - From the down bay, No. 82008 leaves for Sidmouth and Exmouth with holidaymakers travelling in pre-war Maunsell and post-war Bullied stock on a Sunday service in August 1962. For the through services this was an awkward arrangement, as the branch joined the down main line in the opposite direction to that which most long distance trains took, necessitating the blocking of the through lines for all shunting moves as well as for the splitting and joining of trains that took place here.

Right - Steam working ended in 1963, a DMU service then provided until closure to passengers on 6 March 1967. Freight on the branches lasted until the following Summer by which time the main line had already been singled. The recently lifted branch track presents something of a scar on the landscape, the new housing known as 'Feniton Garden Village' being intended for commuters but by now with no station to commute from. Eventually local pressure together with a more enlightened approach prevailed and the former Sidmouth Junction was reopened as 'Feniton' on 3 May 1971. There is still considerable commuter traffic on this line and with construction now started on the new town of Cranbrook on flood plains near the airport, Exeter is set to see a further increase in the local rail infrastructure. (Tony Woodforth)

TIPTON ST JOHNS

Tipton St Johns is a small village, in the middle of which was a level crossing next to the station. In the days before everyday car usage, this would have been inconvenient, but latterly it would cause many a frayed temper. Tipton was another point where trains were split- for Sidmouth or Exmouth via Budleigh - or joined from the aforementioned, to form a through service after reversal and further shunting, at Sidmouth Junction. Much of this shunting also involved the need for the engine to run round and propel its stock on to that which was to form the leading half of the train. All this meant a necessity at keeping the gates shut to road traffic for 15-20 minutes, a trial for both road and rail user. In this June 1959 shot, the Exmouth coaches are about to buffer up to the Sidmouth portion, before they all depart for Waterloo. (Peter Triggs, col. Amyas Crump)

Tipton St Johns after closure. The main station building survives today, having been converted to living accommodation. A bungalow has been attached at the far end and part of the platform survives but there is little evidence that this was once a busy little junction. Today the East Devon resorts retain their air of exclusivity and are marketed as being on the 'Jurassic Coast', the cliffs from Lyme Regis to Sidmouth now a World Heritage site in consequence of their Jurassic age strata visible from the beaches below. Villages such as Ottery St Mary (which was the intermediate station between Tipton and the Junction) and Tipton St Johns are also now 'desirable areas', a complete change around compared with their struggling throughout the railway age. (Bernard Wells)

The Sidmouth and Budleigh branches divided immediately beyond the level crossing at Tipton St Johns, the scars of the two lines still evident in the late 1960s. The Sidmouth line is to the right, climbing steeply to a terminus high above the town, enough to discourage all but the most determined day tripper. In consequence it has retained its 'select' image as per Victorian days. Strange to relate also that freight would outlive passenger working by a couple of months.

The Budleigh line, running along the flat valley floor, came later, converting sleepy Tipton St Johns from the least important station on the Sidmouth Railway into an occasionally-busy little junction, although it never acquired that suffix to its name.
(Tony Woodforth)

SIDMOUTH

closed (p) 6-3-67 (g) 8-5-67

When BR was reorganised in 1963 the Southern lines west of Salisbury were passed into Western Region care. Three months later Dr Beeching made his pronouncement that most should go, hence it was left to the Western Region to administer the last rights. As we have already seen, in many places the WR quickly banished Southern locomotives and substituted their own machines. With closure pending came the enthusiasts tours, including the 'The East Devon Railtour', Pannier No. 4666 seen at Sidmouth with the first part of the trip, 28 February 1965. (The second part ran exactly one week later.) Each tour was split into two, one to Sidmouth the second to Lyme Regis. The 7 March outing destined to be the last time a steam hauled train would be shunted at both Sidmouth Junction and Tipton St Johns.

Budleigh Salterton was the main intermediate station on the line from Tipton St Johns to Exmouth line, which initially terminated here from 1897 before extension to Exmouth in 1903 by the LSWR. These lines, worked as one, closed to passengers at the same time as the Sidmouth branch and all structures were demolished. At Budleigh Salterton's main station (further on there was also a single-platform station at East Budleigh), the station offices were soon pitched into the former trackbed and Messrs. Norman's Removals and Storage warehouse was erected on the site of the old goods yard. Today even Norman's has gone, remembered in the name of the road serving the new houses as 'Norman Crescent' and the 'superior development' on the actual station site, 'Norman Mews'. One can still photograph these properties from the Leas Road bridge parapet at the east end of the station, which remains today as the sole evidence that a railway once ran through here. Ironic perhaps the short lived successor should be commemorated more than the longer lived railway. But then it is often preferred to try and obliterate any reference to a railway ever having existed. (Both: Tony Woodforth)

SR EXMOUTH branch

EXMOUTH

With the loss of the Budleigh route and the future apparently secure for the Topsham line, there was a continuing need for a station, but on a much lesser scale than the four platforms, engine shed, extensive yard and harbour branch of its heyday. This seaside resort with a sea of dereliction, can have done little to help the local tourism trade, but it was seven years before construction of the new station got under way in 1975. The new facilities, along the lines of a slightly enlarged bus stop, is on the site of the old platform two - to the left of the rather thoughtful looking young lady. Rather like Ilfracombe, those long platforms built for excursion trains looked particularly desolate and deserted when occupied by a three car, or less, diesel unit. (Both: Chris Henley, col. Amyas Crump)

Exmouth station has been described as a 'miniature Waterloo', as it had (and still has) a busy commuter traffic to Exeter. To reinforce this impression, the latticework gates at the ends of the platforms saw the only sets of steam-hauled BR suburban stock on the SR outside of London, hauled by BR Standard class 3 tanks. In WR controlled years, DMUs served the commuter alone as the holiday trains of the steam era were long gone. Today the frequent service still resembles traffic of the Capital, but Exmouth station looks more like a bus stop.

EXETER CENTRAL

Exeter Central was the focal point for the Southern system in the south west, where many trains were joined or split, it was the terminus for Exmouth services and summit of the epic climb from St Davids station, providing one of the greatest spectacles of the power of steam with, typically, two engines leading and two more banking - around 100,000lbs of tractive effort working flat out. Having worked the train down from Westbury on one occasion an ex GW 47xx worked through to Central causing great consternation as they were prohibited. Imagine the outcry today at the idea of a railway station being built in the moat of an historic castle, giving a surprisingly rural feel to a city centre location. In the goods yard, Blue Circle cement traffic is buoyant and which survived the end of steam. The facilities here had been completely rebuilt by the Southern Railway in the 1930s, but further plans for a flyover and high level station at St Davids came to naught. The iron trainshed structure formerly here was moved to Exmouth Junction as a cover for part of the SR Concrete Works, that site later being used by the coal distribution centre when concrete manufacture was instead concentrated at Taunton. (Tony Woodforth)

Exeter St Davids, whilst purely GWR in origin, was an important part of the Southern as well. Dropping cautiously down the 1 in 37 bank to St Davids from Central is Standard Class 5 No. 73044 piloted by a Warship class diesel hydraulic in what is a scene of great historical interest. Working from left to right, Exeter West Signal Box was moved to Crewe Heritage Centre after the introduction of the Exeter MAS scheme in the 1980s. Beyond, the water tank sits on top of the old South Devon Railway atmospheric pump house, used for many years as a gas works for carriage lighting, restaurant cars etc. Normally shed water tanks were put on top of the coal stage - the central brick building attended by a D63xx and largely hidden by the canopy is the loco shed. Going back to the construction of the main line, the west end of the station at St Davids Junction marked the end-on junction of the Bristol & Exeter and the South Devon Railways. The carriage sheds and associated tracks were always known as South Devon sidings with the carriage sheds themselves being of very similar design to the familiar wooden train sheds at Ashburton and Moretonhampstead. Within the carriage sheds lie spare stock, including at least one of the 1950s built auto trailers familiar on those lines. Marking the change in ownership of the land was a granite boundary marker inscribed 'SDR' in the grass by the redundant 'Cordon' gas tank wagon at far right; the last use for this gas tank would have been to supply the ex Barry Railway coaching stock used on the Culm Valley Branch.

On summer Saturdays Exeter St Davids was so busy that Teign Valley services were terminated at Alphington Halt, passengers having to take local buses to and from the city. This was the only alternative route the GWR owned for diversions when the main line along the sea wall at Dawlish was closed after storms but was not suitable for the heaviest locomotives. Thus the GWR and SR had arrangements for each to work trains to Plymouth via the other's line in the event of disruption and had regular workings over each others' routes to keep crews signed for the 'other' road.

ASHTON

Ashton, recently repainted yet only days before closure **(right)** and again a little later having been converted into a house **(below).** This had been the original, rather modest terminal of the passenger services on the Teign Valley Branch, hence the loco shed a little way beyond the station. This was closed in Edwardian times but the building survived until after closure of the line. Freight was always the principle traffic, and as built there was a freight only extension to just short of the later site of Christow station. From Exeter Railway Junction (just west

of St Thomas station, Exeter) to what had been known as Teign House Siding opened on 1 July 1903.

Ashton had been host to another of the popular camping coaches. The level crossing was controlled by an exposed two lever frame with a standard pattern sign mounted on two lengths of bridge rail.

TRUSHAM

The picturesque Teign Valley carried a considerable mineral traffic, particularly roadstone from the many private sidings and loading points along the valley. Transhipment costs encouraged the switch to road haulage but even so nowadays most of those same quarries lie silent and deserted. Transhipment would have been a different sort of problem in the beginning as this line was built to standard gauge but connected with the Moretonhampstead Branch which remained broad gauge only until the great conversion weekend of May 1892 when all remaining bg track West of Exeter was narrowed. As at Ashton, there was a modest level of agricultural traffic with milk in churns going from local farms to the Creamery at Totnes by rail. Floods in September 1960 washed away the alignment north of here and for a time Trusham was the terminus of a thrice weekly freight which had been running to Christow.

CHUDLEIGH

I visited here with fellow members of the Great Western Society after going on my first rail tour, to Bovey. The wooden buildings remained in their ex GW dark and light stone to the end. Having been forced to accept a lower level alignment than desired, there were consequently a number occasions when the station flooded and passengers had to alight at the 'flood platform' a short distance beyond the overbridge seen in this view. The pagoda shelter along with the rest of Chudleigh Knighton Halt and its level crossing have long become part of the foundation of the A38, which has also absorbed the trackbed most of the way to Chudleigh station, the site of which is now no more than waterlogged scrub and woodland. However, I was taken aback by the local radio travel news announcing "delays at Chudleigh Station" only recently, over half a century after the service was withdrawn! Perhaps they meant the crossroads!

HEATHFIELD

Having started as two separate lines of different gauge, the demise of the broad gauge brought them together, so finally the layout shewn here was adopted to allow trains to be more readily diverted from the exposed coastal route. Curving in from the right, trains to or from Exeter had no need for shunting on or off the Moretonhampstead branch link to Newton Abbot, one of the many wartime improvements to our rail network. The goods loop (with load gauge) ran over a wagon weighbridge with a corrugated iron hut. The brick enclosure was the coal bunker of the substantial signalbox which stood this side of it until closure in 1965, when points became hand operated. Freight continued to use the TVR link as a headshunt for banana traffic to the Fyffes depot and access to the bay platform (off picture to the right). The timber station buildings burnt down in the late 1970s: although strangely a 'Beware of Trains' would survive for a further decade.

Currently, the only rail use of the site is to run round timber wagons of the Chirk service from Teigngrace, the Gulf oil traffic which sustained it for most of the rest of the 20th Century, and its track, having gone for ever.

Heathfield with one of the shuttles on the Enthusiasts Special of 5 July 1970, this backwater being visited by other tours since including an HST from Buckfastleigh and most recently, the "142 Farewell Tour" on 27 November 2011. Opened in 1874 when the Teign Valley branch started it was originally called 'Chudleigh Road', but changed to Heathfield in October 1882. The layout at Heathfield station was altered and extended in 1927, complete with the installation of electric lighting. In 1972 just one of the pair of pipes once used as flower pot's remains outside the waiting room door, these are from the adjacent brick & tile works. Notice also how the Teign Valley company used a very similar design of buildings at Chudleigh.

GWR *MORETONHAMPSTEAD branch*

BOVEY closed (p) 28-2-59 (g) 5-7-70

A complete set of buildings still in GW paint and yet we still took pictures of the DMU! How much more there must have been to admire, had we thought to look closer. We all saw a BR van marooned in the yard, but few noticed that the goods shed door slid on rails marked M & SDR (Moretonhampstead & South Devon Railway) which dated back to the building of the line. This is one of the last day shuttles of 5 July 1970, waiting to return to Newton Abbot. The branch was then further curtailed to the Gulf oil sidings north of Heathfield, opened in June 1965. The trackbed from Bovey Pottery and Granite sidings, (for the Haytor Granite Tramway) through Brimley Halt, Bovey and on towards Lustleigh has now been covered by the Bovey Tracey bypass. Fortunately, some materials were salvaged for use on the current South Devon Railway and the station buildings display something of the history of the locality including relics from the station.

LUSTLEIGH

On the last day of service, 28 February 1959, the sun shines on the bracken as former GWR Prairie No, 5196 brings the 09.20 from Newton Abbott through delightful moorland colour on the approach to Lustleigh. It is obvious that the local track gang were not going to let the future of the line affect the standard of track maintenance, which of the highest order. No. 5196, along with 5195, had been allocated to Newton Abbot whose trademark polished safety valve cover (and copper chimney cap) are evident. With the reduction in work brought about by the loss of passenger trains on this line and the Teign Valley, No. 5196 was withdrawn at the end of the year and fourteen months after this picture, had been reduced to a pile of scrap at Swindon Works. Many locals doubted the finality of the closure, having heard talk of excursions being run and the possibility of diesels being used to restart a future service. Closure day also marked the end for five intermediate stations on the mainline between Newton Abbot and Plymouth; these were Wrangaton, Bittaford Platform, Ivybridge, Cornwood and Plympton.

PULLABROOK HALT

Pullabrook Halt had opened for the summer of 1931 under the name Hawkmoor Halt, a time when the GWR Publicity Department were very active in the promotion of hiking holidays and excursions for walkers, Hawkmoor being one of the many places on the GWR from which to explore. After the number of patients for the Hawkmoor Sanatorium (some two miles down the lanes) had tailed off, the name was changed in 1955. Track north of Bovey was removed in 1966.

Having climbed on through Lustleigh, and crossed the main road on bridges that were ever more of a bottleneck for road users, trains arrived at the gas-lit terminus where the overall roof would provide welcome shelter from moorland weather. .No. 1466 (later preserved by the Great Western Society, Didcot) was a regular for the auto worked trains but, with no 14xx available on this occasion in June 1958, a small prairie has been provided. The trainshed did not last long after closure, but the stone offices and the nameboard remained, at least to the mid 1960s, in ever more derelict condition.

MANOR HOUSE HOTEL
MORETONHAMPSTEAD
NORTH BOVEY
DEVON
GWR

Sunshine has found a gap in the cloud to once again highlight the colour of the bracken of the moorland backdrop. The whole site has been taken over by Thompsons whose red lorries have long been a familiar sight. When this railhead provided distribution facilities for the local and wider agricultural communities, extensive warehouses were provided for the much smaller vehicles used. Beyond these the former engine shed doorway displays the generous proportions of its broad gauge origin.

The GWR acquired the Manor House Hotel at Moretonhampstead and had it extended in the 1930s. Renowned for its golf course and extensive fishing rights, it was used as a hospital during WW2 thus bringing LNER B12s to Dartmoor on ambulance trains. Post-war the Great Western planned to invest in and expand, its group of hotels, but railway nationalisation brought the decision to separate off all integrated but non-rail activities. After several changes in its fortunes, and now known as the Bovey Castle, the hotel is thriving and the grounds are well cared for. Some years ago I was fortunate enough to be able to arrange a behind the scenes tour. Our willing guide was perplexed that we had no interest in the newly refurbished rooms, but wanted to look in the cellars and broom cupboards. (The visit being on behalf of the Great Western Trust at Didcot.)

Moretonhampstead was laid out as a through station with the intention that the line should be extended to Chagford, a prosperous town but across typical Dartmoor terrain. The coming of the motor bus provided a much more cost effective alternative and an early GWR Milnes-Daimler is posed outside Rock House at Chagford, the latter serving as both the District Office and depot, on a route which started in April 1906. With suitable input from the Publicity Dept at Paddington, services ran locally to Becky Falls, Haytor, Moretonhampstead, Paignton, Princetown and Totnes, and there was also a 'motor' for the conveyance of the Hotel guests to and from the station. In 1929 operation of the GWR bus fleet - over two hundred vehicles - was transferred to Western National, Devon General and other local companies across the system. Rock House still retains the atmosphere of its past role, but no road motors have occupied its garage or been serviced over the open air inspection pit for a very long time. Elsewhere one GWR 'railmotor' has recently seen the completion of its long term restoration to a very high standard. (Photo courtesy of Rendells Estate Agents)

TEIGNGRACE

Teigngrace. The cast iron nameboard on the left gained the add-on 'HALT' having become unstaffed in May 1939. Twenty nine years later, the halt with the former station offices, presents a very sad sight. Closure to passengers in March 1959 was not regarded as the end by locals. The South Devon Railway Preservation Society was set up, based at Teigngrace station offices, it campaigned harder than the Town Councils. The latter were accepting the Transport Commission undertaking to review the closure when cheaper diesel units became available. Likewise, many locals didn't bother to travel 'the last train' because they didn't believe it would be the last. Teigngrace station dated from 1867. There were also a number of clay loading points along the branch. Having been dormant for several years, a new flow started recently for timber from one of these at nearby Teignbridge to Chirk.

Left - The derelict platform at Teigngrace still displays the cut-away in the coping stones which were made to accommodate the swing of GWR locomotive cylinders.

(86) S. D. R.

Passenger's Luggage.

Staverton to

TEIGNGRACE

Newton Abbot was very much a railway town, although the former works are out of shot in this view of the west end in 1972 when the only movement was an '08' with Naval Bedford trucks and also concrete sections for the Engineers Dept. The background is dominated by the coal fired power station which was rail connected until 1968. Wide, lengthy platforms and offices opened by Lord Mildmay of Fleet, show how important this busy junction was when the new station opened in 1927. Like many other enthusiasts, I have happy memories of the 'relic shop' that once existed in a hut on the platform here, where a considerable number of totem signs could be seen. The loco shed, closed to steam in June 1962, still houses a two-tone green class 47 on this occasion, but windows are smashed in the new amenity block. All the diesel servicing, stabling and repair having been moved to Plymouth Laira, the last allocation of Warship class diesel hydraulics being withdrawn or moved away in January 1972. Afterwards vegetation soon took hold on the wasteland formerly occupied by the shed and works. By the time redevelopment came earlier this century, the town had lost its connection with the railway and so no attempt was made to investigate its archeological potential. The fact that the whole loco shed was built on a raft of unused bridge rail (as used on the broad gauge), was not discovered until it was too late to stop the last of it being broken up for scrap. The Contractors had no interest in history either, and so your author derived a certain satisfaction from shewing them a GWR map of the WW2 air raid on the station, which indicated a 250kg unexploded bomb immediately under the location of their site office!

GWR *TOTNES QUAY branch* *closed 7-12-69*

The three-quarter mile line to Totnes Quay, opened 10 November 1873, diverged just east of the station at Totnes opposite the branch to Ashburton. Until 1948 the town end of the branch was horse-worked, having crossed the main street of the town at Tram Gate; thereafter a road tractor performed the shunting. Traffic included imported timber and Messrs. Symonds Cyder had an office here.

Cattle traffic was quite extensive and the cattle dock and part of the Quay line formed the first base of the embryonic Great Western Society before their eventual move to Didcot in December 1967. Seen here is preserved No. 1369 stored for a time at Totnes but now on the 'South Devon Railway' at Buckfastleigh.

BUCKFASTLEIGH   closed (p) 1-11-58 (g) 7-9-62   reopened 5-4-69

Another line where locals had their own name for the service was the Dart Valley where it was known as 'Bulliver' - presumed to be an affectionate corruption of Kipling's 'Bolivar'. Buckfast, like Ashburton, has always been an important place but had a very circuitous rail journey to the commercial centre of Newton Abbot although reached quite readily by road. The branch passenger service succumbed on 1 November 1958 the last train requiring Nos. 1466 and 1470. With the line still open for freight, the 'Buckfastleigh Combined Sunday Schools' annual excursion - another double headed working - ran for a further four years until complete closure on 7 September 1962. In this pre-closure view, a camp coach from the Dean era (notice the clerestory) would not see much more use. Again the station is in the livery of its pre-nationalisation owners and one that it still bears in preservation, having been (officially) reopened by the late Dr Richard Beeching on 2 May 1969, although trains had started running on the last day of the tax year, 5 April.

ASHBURTON   closed (p) 1-11-58 (g) 7-9-62

Ashburton displaying the wooden overall roof for which it was so well known, very similar to those at Moretonhampstead, Kingswear and Frome, although so far no clear photo of the one at Tiverton from 1848-84 has come to light. Quarterly cattle fairs were held generating a considerable traffic for the railway, but a nightmare for the staff - on one occasion two engines being blocked in by the cramped layout here. On a much quieter day No. 1472 simmers in the sunshine and is rightly being admired by a group of young people. When closure came, the loco was redundant and moved to Weymouth for a spell. With more closures came transfer to Gloucester and use on the last trains to Kemble, Tetbury and Chalford, No 1472 destined to become one of the last four of the class in service. The other three would survive in preservation, not so No. 1472 which was lost to scrap merchants Messrs. Cashmores at Newport.

The station is seen again but now under restoration, with, appropriately, an Austin A40 Devon in the yard. To replace the missing signs, some were acquired from Tiverton, as seen in the earlier picture of the last train there. Unfortunately Ashburton never fully reopened under its preservation era owners, the trackbed from here to Buckfastleigh being earmarked for the new alignment of the A38 trunk road. Thus the battle for preservation was lost and the branch cut back to Buckfastleigh in 1971 to allow construction of the A38 on that section of the trackbed. The station then became part of a garage and has recently been in the news once more, with talk of yet another supermarket.

ASHBURTON

What might have been. Ashburton when hopes ran high. Perhaps this is the ultimate example of an 'Impermanent Way', one that had so much potential but was lost to the then-mighty steamroller of the road lobby. Surely Ashburton was a victim of its timing, for who would expect such a priceless relic of our great industrial heritage to be swept away in that fashion today? However, what remains now may still suffer its final fate in the face of the equivalent of the road lobby today, the great supermarkets, which ride roughshod over the wishes of mere local citizens. (Sean Bolan)

GWR KINGSWEAR branch

CHURSTON
closed (g) 4-12-67

A station that I used only once - by accident. In 1969 I was given a day off school to escort my mother to a venue just outside Paignton, the plan being to alight at Goodrington Sands Halt. On arrival there I announced that it was time to get off, my mother steadfastly refused as "It couldn't be a proper station, there were no Porters in sight" and so the DMU moved off and we caught the Devon General bus back from Churston, by then a very bleak and desolate station. Here the loop and signalbox were taken out of use on 20 December 1963 but subsequently reinstated after the 'Dart Valley Railway Company' took over the line from Paignton to Kingswear at the end of 1972. The Association of Train Operating Companies has ambitions of running services as far as Churston in order to serve Brixham (see overleaf), whose own two-mile line closed in 1963, this according to plans laid out in 2009.
(Sean Bolan)

The auto-worked 'Brixham Whippet' last worked on 4 March 1961, being replaced by a single unit diesel railcar the following Monday. Still hauling a trailing load of fish as required, this is one of the last steam workings with loco No. 1466 in charge. With the loss of work for the auto engines locally, No. 1466 moved to Exeter for use on the Culm Valley, Exe Valley and Tivvy Bumper services before being withdrawn and sold, becoming the first locomotive to be owned by the Great Western Society and at that time based on the Totnes Quay branch.

The Brixham fish traffic was considerable with seasonal increases often requiring additional trains as well as when holidaymakers brought seasonal influxes - then the well-cleaned fish vans were used to convey some of the additional luggage - doubtless providing an additional lasting memory of the holiday! The final Brixham - Churston train ran on 11 May 1963, a few weeks after Dr. Beeching's Report, but the summer timetables shewed an enhanced service....! Life returned briefly to the branch that summer as a film-set, for the Michael Winner film 'The System' for which Brixham became 'Roxham'. The rails were lifted soon after filmed ceased and by the end of 1966 the buildings seen here had been vandalised, then demolished and finally used to create a sizable bonfire. The site thereafter redeveloped for housing.

STEAM FERRY CROSSING

'Steam Ferry Crossing' on the banks of the River Dart estuary, a very Great Western scene with the diminutive box and accompanying GWR built house. Changing names twice still didn't get Kingswear Crossing Halt into the public timetables. The level crossing serves the Dartmouth Higher Ferry, under the ownership of the Paignton & Dartmouth Steam Railway, now 'Britannia Halt' has gone whilst the signal box controls all of the signalling between Paignton and Kingswear.   (Sean Bolan)

KINGSWEAR

Looking towards the stopblocks, this is the basic railway which in 1968 was proposed for closure beyond Paignton. Eventually, agreement was reached whereby the line closed was closed by BR on 31 December 1972 but reopened the next day under the ownership of the steam railway.

Once upon a time this was a hive of activity, the quayside unloading endless cargoes of coal for the short rail journey to Torquay Gas Works, receiving and dispatching the 'Torbay Express' from and to Paddington and in summer dealing with a procession of excursions and through trains. Instead in the scenes on this page there is little or nothing, although in the lower the mini parked outside the station displays evidence of recent nuptials!

KINGSWEAR

Throughout the years traffic had grown necessitating considerable lengthening of the platforms beyond the original trainshed of 1866, welcome news for a line that had been so costly to build. A century later and as was the culture of the time, to justify closure BR ran down the passenger service to end with inconveniently timed slow trains, deliberately it seemed, intended to avoid connections where any transfer might be made.

Opposite bottom right - Around 1900 land was reclaimed from Waterhead Creek to provide further carriage storage sidings, cattle pens and a turntable that had once handled the vast number of tender engines from freight types to Castles and Kings. This land was sold to recoup part of the purchase price of the line. Sadly, the turntable and carriage sidings were lifted before then and the area is now a car park.
(all: Sean Bolan)

DARTMOUTH STATION

Top - Dartmouth was the intended terminus of the branch which ended at Kingswear, but even if it never achieved a railway it did at least get a station complete with a Station Master, such was the importance of the town and its Naval college. By far the best known of the connecting ferries was 'The Mew ' built in Falmouth in 1908 and famed for steaming all the way to Dover in 1940 to try and help with the evacuation of Dunkirk. 'The Mew' finally made her last River Dart crossing in October 1954. Her last refit had been in 1948 from when the fire notice dates but there is very little surviving from the ship, this souvenir being given to an appreciative youngster. MVs 'Humphrey Gilbert' and 'Adrian Gilbert' came as permanent replacements in 1956 and at closure in 1972 the vessels passed initially into local authority ownership, changing hands several times before returning to the Dart. On the waterfront above the ferry is the back of Dartmouth Station and the landing pontoon.

Bottom - Dartmouth, the station that never saw a train. Even so it displays the correct GWR colour scheme and evidence that the roof sign did not always proclaim 'B.R'.

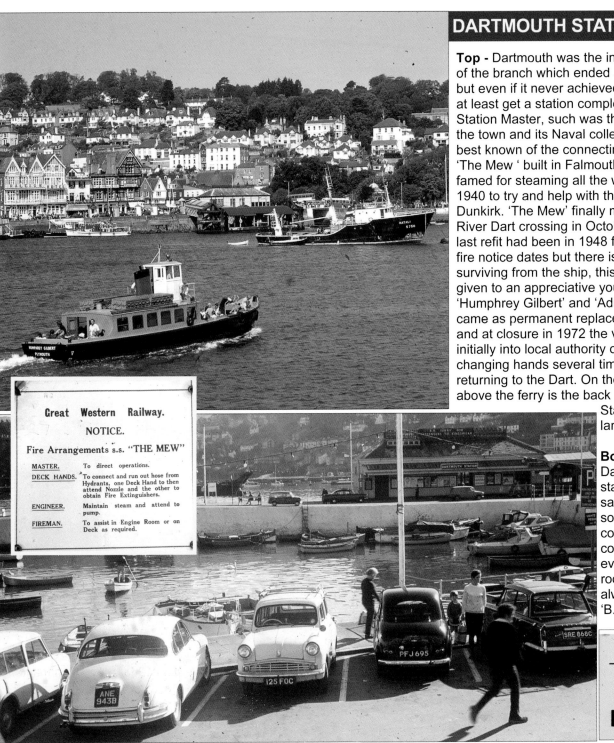

Great Western Railway.

NOTICE.

Fire Arrangements s.s. "THE MEW"

MASTER.	To direct operations.
DECK HANDS.	To connect and run out hose from Hydrants, one Deck Hand to then attend Nozzle and the other to obtain Fire Extinguishers.
ENGINEER.	Maintain steam and attend to pump.
FIREMAN.	To assist in Engine Room or on Deck as required.

B & E R

To

DARTMOUTH.

GARA BRIDGE

eaving the Newton Abbot-Plymouth mainline at South Brent on the southern slopes of Dartmoor, the very picturesque
Kingsbridge Branch ran close to the River Avon for much of the way, providing more idyllic locations for camping coaches.
Change came with dieselisation, no more Paddington - Kingsbridge Saturday through trains giving the branch loco an
pportunity to carry Express headlamps. The familiar story of bad connections to discourage travel have led to a closure
otice going up, seen by the crossing, on 27 March 1962 with complete closure on 14 September 1963. Scrap men made
hort work of the immaculate signalbox, the stone buildings surviving - just - to be developed as a private home.
Sean Bolan)

GARA BRIDGE

5 miles 39 chains from Brent, Gara Bridge was the only crossing station on the branch. Approached via a level crossing the buildings were on a curve - Gara is an ancient Celtic word meaning 'rough'. For many years Camping Coaches were stabled here during the season: today the two platforms are linked across the erstwhile trackbed to form one private residence.

SORLEY TUNNEL

Tunnelling under Sorley Cross took the railway out of the valley of the River Avon, which it had run beside most of the way from Brent, and down into Kingsbridge where the station lay beside the Salcombe Road. During WW2 Sorley Tunnel provided a very welcome refuge for an evening train being pursued by a German bomber, its bomb dropping on top of the tunnel. Luckily, the train escaped unscathed. Following closure, track lifting had started as early as November 1963, the well known contractor George Cohen taking some six months to complete the job. As was so often the case, the track had been relaid quite recently, much of it being sold by Cohen's for reuse rather than scrap.

GREAT WESTERN RAILWAY (135a)

KINGSBRIDGE

TO

No. of Packages | Carriage Paid

Route via EXETER & L.&S.W.R.

The huge rounds of protest, and well loaded summer trains, were, as usual a wasted effort. Since there was so much local support, a preservation attempt was made for the 'Primrose Line' which also gained the backing of the local council. Famously at the end of the meeting a visit was made to the station yard, only to find that the demolition crew had spent the afternoon cutting up the pointwork, rendering preservation unviable. The extensive site close to the town was soon taken up by light industry and transport, the station itself finally being demolished in the summer of 2009, the stonework recovered in the hope that it may be reused at Bere Ferrers. During WW2 General Eisenhower visited Kingsbridge in connection with preparations for the subsequent D-Day landings, this being the nearest station to Slapton Sands - the latter sadly recalled for all the wrong reasons.

SR *DARTMOOR main line*

CREDITON

The Southern route from Exeter to Plymouth around the northern and western slopes of Dartmoor has a colourful, long and complicated history, the section to Meldon still having track and seeing some use, and therefore (some might say) does not fit wholly within the concept of this series. However, there are a few points that certainly merit inclusion. (Crediton had a railway which changed gauge twice during the three-year delay between completion and opening.) The charming buildings here clearly display the Brunelian allegiance of the Exeter & Crediton Railway with a fine example of his Elizabethan roadside style - which currently operates as a tea room. The period shelters remain for passenger use, doubtless few of them stray down the platform far enough to admire the loading dock, now one of the very last places to carry a full broad gauge width stop block with clear evidence of how the line was narrowed - ***well worthy of appreciation!*** For several decades after the LSWR finally gained control, the GWR continued to be a thorn in their side, running a daily goods train to Crediton. That chapter of the story is long closed together with the yard and all other freight facilities along the line, each now given over to commercial businesses and road hauliers.

Heading North from Crediton, the routes to Barnstaple and Okehampton have operated as parallel single lines since Coleford Junction signal box closed in 1971. This is where the former LSWR main line to the west turns away across northern Dartmoor. Bow and North Tawton were provided with sizeable station premises but suffered from being so isolated: by comparison, Sampford Courtenay was much more basic. Beyond the buildings there had been up to five sidings until the yard closed in 1961, the station becoming unstaffed in 1965. For railwaymen though, even after closure of the passenger service, this location retained a vital facility in the form of a public telephone box. In the era before mobile phones and direct communication between drivers and signallers, the phone box here was the only means of summoning assistance should the need arise.

Curiously, although it lost its regular passenger services in 1972, the station has (intermittent) services today. The Dartmoor Railway refurbished the sole remaining platform and started using it in 2002, running trains between here and a platform at Meldon Quarry. From then until 2008 Devon County Council sponsored a First Great Western service on peak Summer Sundays, connecting with the Heritage railway at Okehampton. These ceased but were reinstated the following year.
(J Bennett, col. Amyas Crump)

After an almost continuous climb for the thirty miles from Exeter, Meldon is nearly the summit of the line. For a loaded stone train this meant that once it was on the move, there was usually no need for power to be applied until reaching Cowley Bridge Junction. The return journey could be a very different matter, with the introduction of mechanical grabs and flat bottom 'Grampus' wagons, returning vehicles were often more full than empty! With actual loadings often well in excess of booked figures, the high torque of the Western diesel hydraulics made them popular with enginemen. The quarry had started with the building of the railway in 1874, and been greatly expanded over the years supplying track ballast as well as aggregates to Exmouth Junction Concrete Works. The rather bleak offices carried a 'builder's plate' dating from 1936. Various engines were outstationed at the small concrete engine shed, USA tank No. DS 234 (formerly No. 30072) took over in 1962 from an ancient Adams G6 and went on to become the last BR steam loco working in Devon when replaced by a class 08 diesel in 1966, thereby making a suitable point to break off our tour. The extensive network of lines West of Meldon will be covered more conveniently together with those of Cornwall in a forthcoming volume.

PLYMOUTH *GWR and SR*

The railways of Plymouth, both Great Western and Southern as well as independent could almost create sufficient material for a volume on their own. In two pages we cannot hope to do justice to this area. Suffice to say the sad remains of the GWR Mill Bay station seen above create a poignant taster for what will follow in the second part of this 'Devon - Cornwall' series (see inside rear cover).

Right - Although no longer railway related, offices near the Barbican in Plymouth still display evidence of previous LSWR ownership. (Sean Bolan)

With the closure of the Okehampton -Tavistock – Bere Alston section of the former SR main line from 6 May 1968, vast swathes of the Southern network in Plymouth also became redundant. This is Ford Viaduct near Devonport. As services to Cornwall have always been so closely linked to Plymouth, a further volume will look again at Plymouth and its branches, along with the closed lines of Cornwall. (Patrick Miller)